OUR GOVERNMENT

The House of Representatives

Fountaindale Public Library
Bolingbrook, IL
(630) 759-2102

by Mari Schuh

BLASTOFF! READERS

BELLWETHER MEDIA • MINNEAPOLIS, MN

Blastoff! Readers are carefully developed by literacy experts to build reading stamina and move students toward fluency by combining standards-based content with developmentally appropriate text.

 Level 1 provides the most support through repetition of high-frequency words, light text, predictable sentence patterns, and strong visual support.

 Level 2 offers early readers a bit more challenge through varied sentences, increased text load, and text-supportive special features.

 **Level 3** advances early-fluent readers toward fluency through increased text load, less reliance on photos, advancing concepts, longer sentences, and more complex special features.

★ **Blastoff! Universe**

Reading Level

Grade **K**

Grades **1–3**

Grade **4**

This edition first published in 2021 by Bellwether Media, Inc.

No part of this publication may be reproduced in whole or in part without written permission of the publisher. For information regarding permission, write to Bellwether Media, Inc., Attention: Permissions Department, 6012 Blue Circle Drive, Minnetonka, MN 55343.

Library of Congress Cataloging-in-Publication Data

Names: Schuh, Mari C., 1975- author.
Title: The House of Representatives / Mari Schuh.
Description: Minneapolis, MN : Bellwether Media, 2021. | Series: Blastoff! readers. Our government | Includes bibliographical references and index. | Audience: Ages 5-8 | Audience: Grades K-1 | Summary: "Developed by literacy experts for students in kindergarten through grade three, this book introduces the House of Representatives to young readers through leveled text and related photos"–Provided by publisher.
Identifiers: LCCN 2019059311 (print) | LCCN 2019059312 (ebook) | ISBN 9781644872024 (library binding) | ISBN 9781681038261 (paperback) | ISBN 9781618919601 (ebook)
Subjects: LCSH: United States. Congress. House–Juvenile literature.
Classification: LCC JK1319 .S359 2021 (print) | LCC JK1319 (ebook) | DDC 328.73/072–dc23
LC record available at https://lccn.loc.gov/2019059311
LC ebook record available at https://lccn.loc.gov/2019059312

Editor: Rebecca Sabelko   Designer: Laura Sowers

Printed in the United States of America, North Mankato, MN.

Table of Contents

What Is the House of Representatives?

The House of Representatives is part of **Congress**. It is often called the House.

meeting of Congress

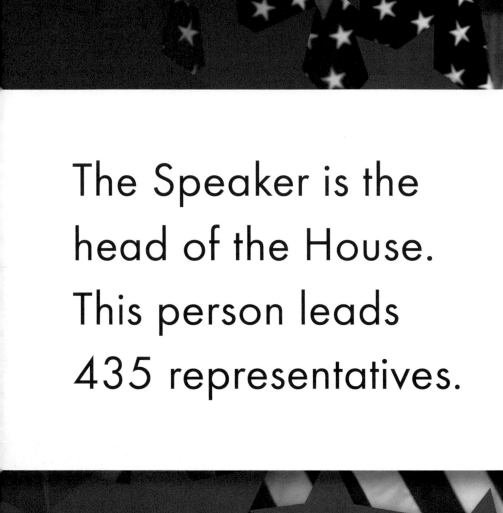

The Speaker is the head of the House. This person leads 435 representatives.

Speaker
Nancy Pelosi

House members
work for their states.
Each member serves
a two-year **term**.

Must Haves

- ✓ **25 or older**
- ✓ **citizen at least seven years**
- ✓ **lives in their state**

Representative Ilhan Omar

Some states have
a lot of people.
These states have
more representatives.

California representatives
Nancy Pelosi   Adam Schiff

#RESIST
MARCH
AN LA PRIDE PROJECT

ResistMarch.org

House members work
in the Capitol building.
It is in Washington, D.C.

Capitol building, Washington, D.C.

Duties

House members help make **laws**. They write new **bills**.

Working Together

Legislative Branch	Executive Branch	Judicial Branch
writes laws	signs laws	studies laws

president

vice president

Senate   House of Representatives

Supreme Court

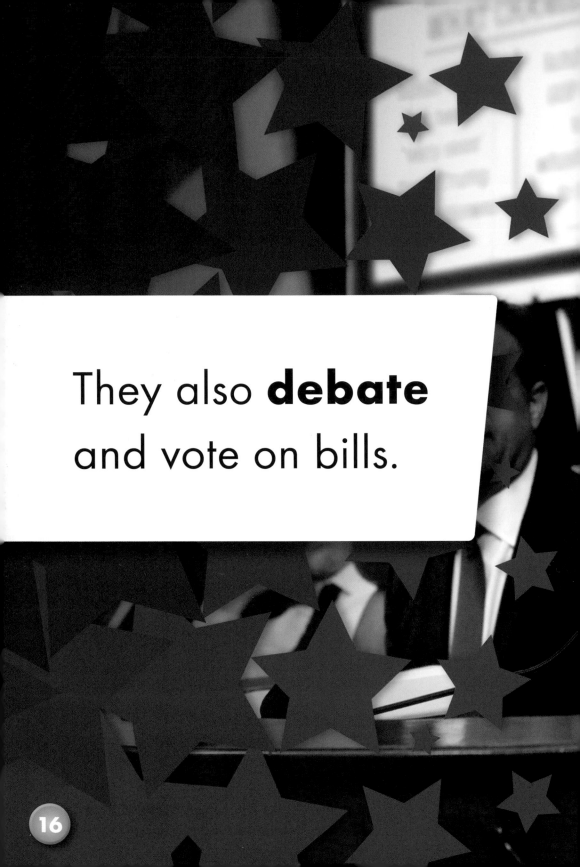

They also **debate** and vote on bills.

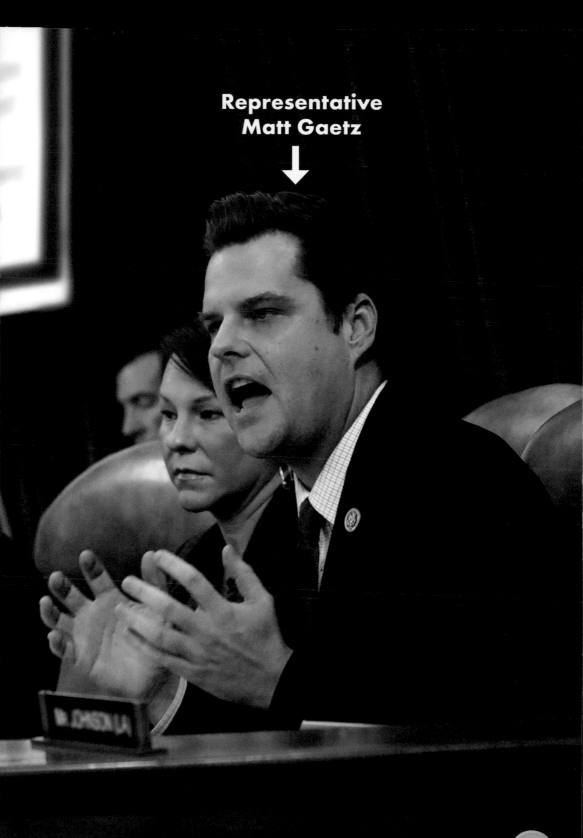

Representative
Matt Gaetz
↓

An Important Job

House members meet with **citizens**. They learn what people need.

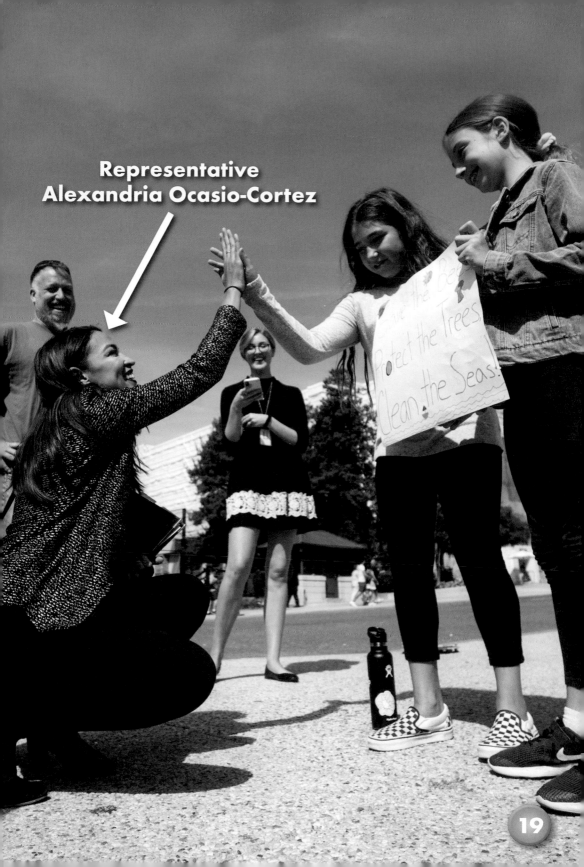

Representative Alexandria Ocasio-Cortez

The House of
Representatives
works for the people!

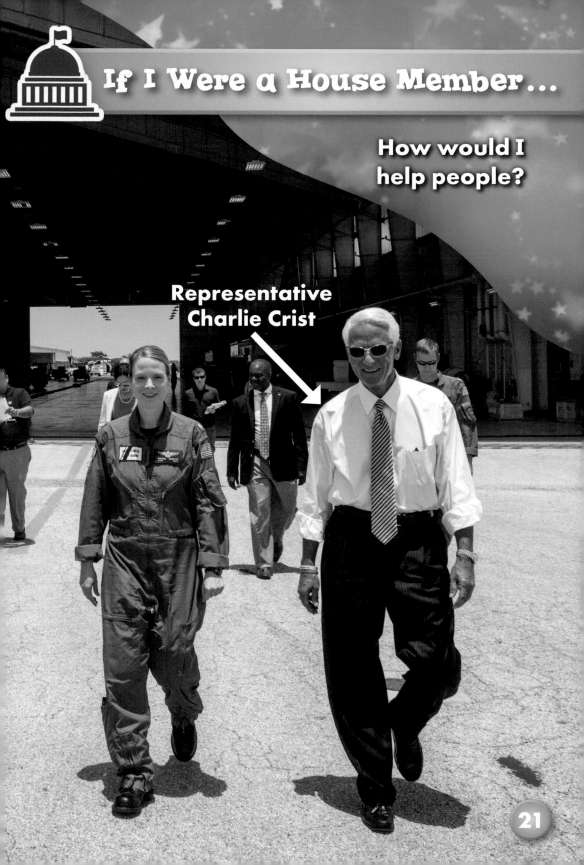

How would I help people?

Representative Charlie Crist

Glossary

bills

written ideas for new laws

debate

to talk about a topic and offer different thoughts

citizens

members of a country

laws

rules that people must follow

Congress

the part of the government that makes laws

term

a fixed period of time

To Learn More

AT THE LIBRARY

Alexander, Vincent. *Legislative Branch.*
Minneapolis, Minn.: Jump!, 2019.

Kortuem, Amy. *The U.S. House of
Representatives.* North Mankato, Minn.:
Capstone Press, 2020.

Schuh, Mari. *The United States Constitution.*
Minneapolis, Minn.: Bellwether Media, 2019.

ON THE WEB

FACTSURFER

Factsurfer.com gives you
a safe, fun way to find
more information.

1. Go to www.factsurfer.com.

2. Enter "House of Representatives" into the
   search box and click 🔍.

3. Select your book cover to see a list of
   related content.

Index